I0824867
RATTLESNAKES
Jessica Coupé
The World of Snakes
AV2
www.av2books.com

Step 1
Go to **www.av2books.com**

Step 2
Enter this unique code
HODAXZQ35

Step 3
Explore your interactive eBook!

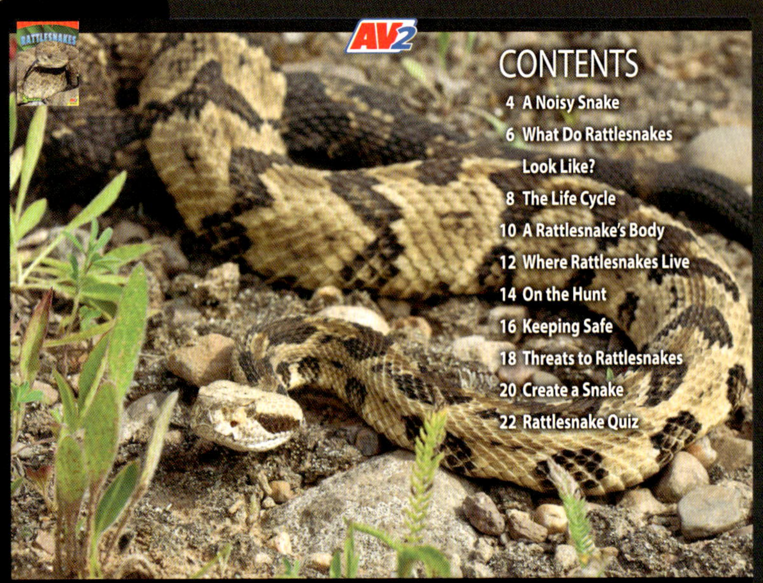

AV2 is optimized for use on any device

Your interactive eBook comes with...

Contents
Browse a live contents page to easily navigate through resources

Audio
Listen to sections of the book read aloud

Videos
Watch informative video clips

Weblinks
Gain additional information for research

Slideshows
View images and captions

Try This!
Complete activities and hands-on experiments

Key Words
Study vocabulary, and complete a matching word activity

Quizzes
Test your knowledge

Share
Share titles within your Learning Management System (LMS) or Library Circulation System

Citation
Create bibliographical references following the Chicago Manual of Style

This title is part of our AV2 digital subscription

1-Year 3–8 Subscription
ISBN 978-1-7911-3306-1

Access hundreds of AV2 titles with our digital subscription.
Sign up for a FREE trial at **www.av2books.com/trial**

RATTLESNAKES

CONTENTS

A Noisy Snake

Rattlesnakes are some of the best-known snakes in the world. They are named for the rattle on their tails. Rattlesnakes are part of the pit viper family. Pit vipers are a group of snakes that use **venom** to hunt. Snakes such as the copperhead and the eyelash viper are also members of this family.

WARNING

Rattlesnake bites are dangerous. **Between 50 and 75 percent** of rattlesnake bites contain venom.

Rattlesnakes are reptiles. All reptiles have scales on their bodies. They are also **cold-blooded**. This means they cannot get warm on their own. They need to use the Sun's heat. In the summer, rattlesnakes rest in cool burrows or under rocks. In the winter, they **hibernate** with other rattlesnakes in underground dens.

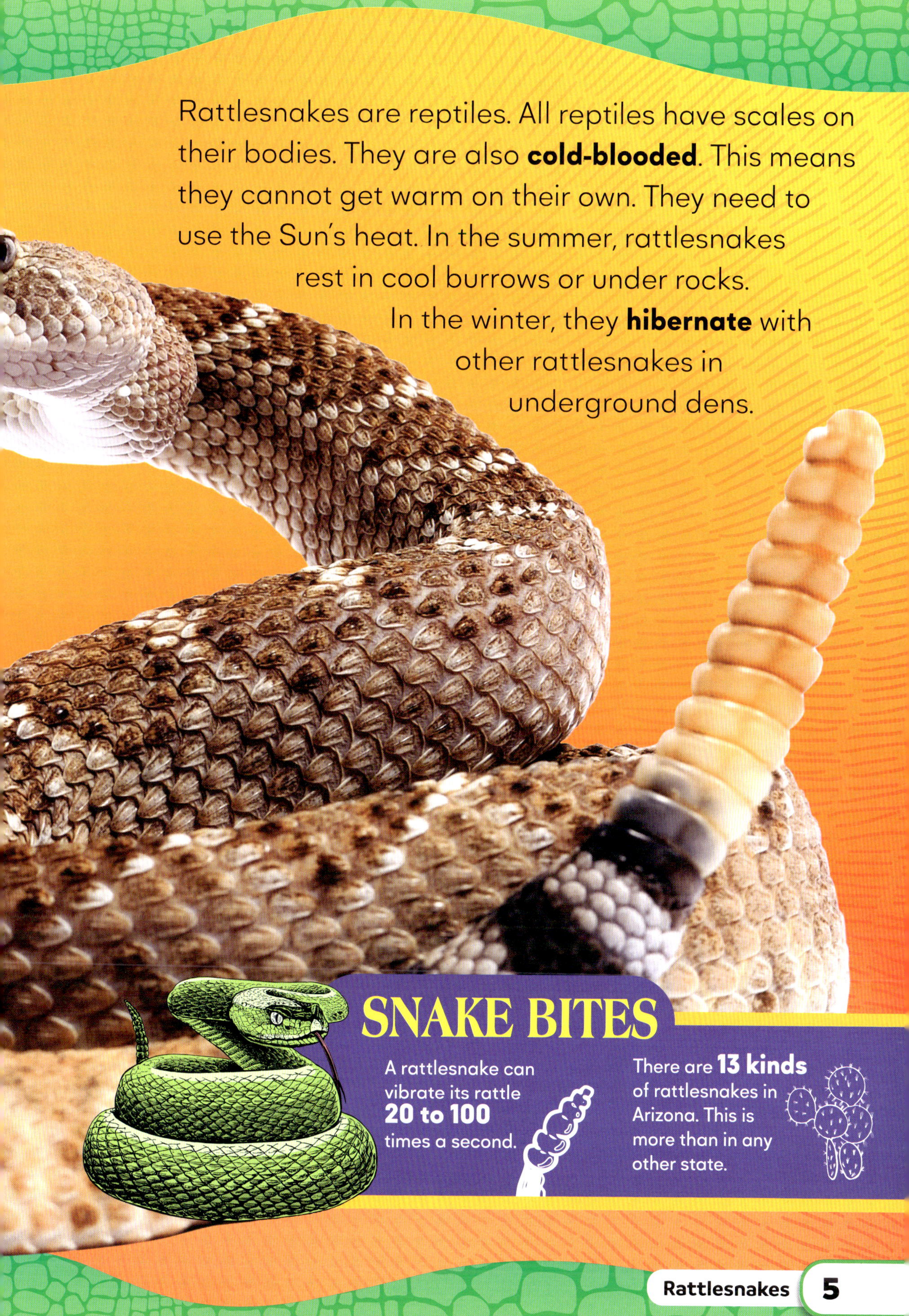

SNAKE BITES

A rattlesnake can vibrate its rattle **20 to 100** times a second.

There are **13 kinds** of rattlesnakes in Arizona. This is more than in any other state.

What Do Rattlesnakes Look Like?

Rattlesnakes have long bodies. Their heads are triangle shaped. The shortest rattlesnake is about 1.6 feet (0.5 meters) long. Eastern diamondbacks are the biggest rattlesnakes. They can grow more than 6 feet (1.8 m) long.

Measuring Up

Average snake lengths

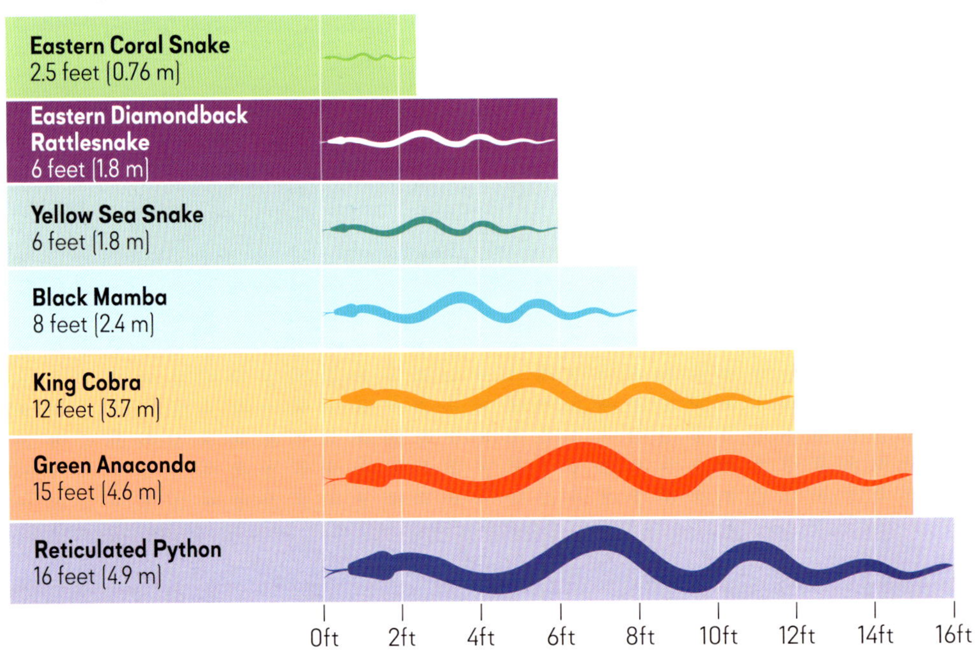

Rattlesnakes come in several colors. These include brown, gray, green, orange, and pink. Rattlesnakes have patterns on their bodies. Some **species**, such as the eastern diamondback, have a diamond pattern on their backs. Other rattlesnakes have different shapes, blotches, or stripes.

A rattlesnake's patterns and colors will often match its surroundings, making the snake seem invisible. The patterns and colors help protect the rattlesnake from **predators**.

The Life Cycle

Like all living things, rattlesnakes have a life cycle. A rattlesnake will be born, grow, and **reproduce**. A rattlesnake may live as long as 20 years.

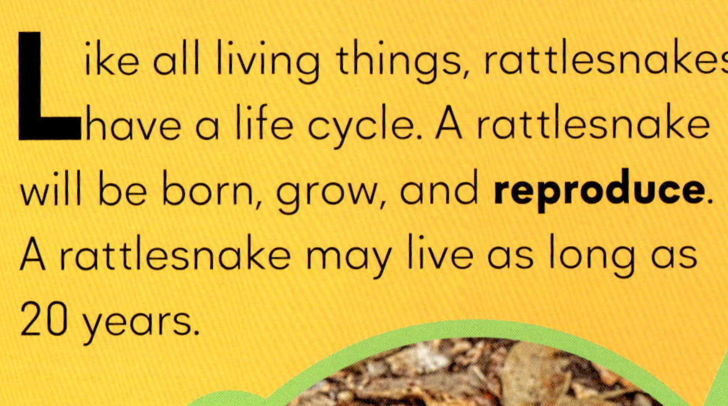

1

A rattlesnake mother does not lay eggs. Instead, she gives birth to between 4 and 10 live young. They are born in late summer.

2

Baby rattlesnakes do not have a rattle on their tail when they are born. They have a button. After shedding their skin, rattlesnakes gain their first rattle **segment**.

3

A young rattlesnake hunts and eats small animals such as lizards. Its rattle grows each time it sheds its skin.

4

Adult male rattlesnakes look for a **mate** when they are 3 or 4 years old. They will compete for a female by wrestling each other. Rattlesnakes mate in the spring.

A Rattlesnake's Body

Like all living things, a rattlesnake has many different **adaptations**. Some keep the snake safe. Others help it to survive in its **habitat**.

Fangs
Rattlesnakes have sharp **fangs**. The fangs fold up against the roof of the mouth when not in use.

Heat Pits
Rattlesnakes have heat-sensing pits between their eyes and nostrils. The heat pits help them find food.

Tongue
Rattlesnakes use their forked tongues to pick up odors on the ground. This helps them hunt for food.
Rattle
The rattle is used as a warning. It is made from **keratin**. This is the same material that makes human hair and fingernails.

Where Rattlesnakes Live

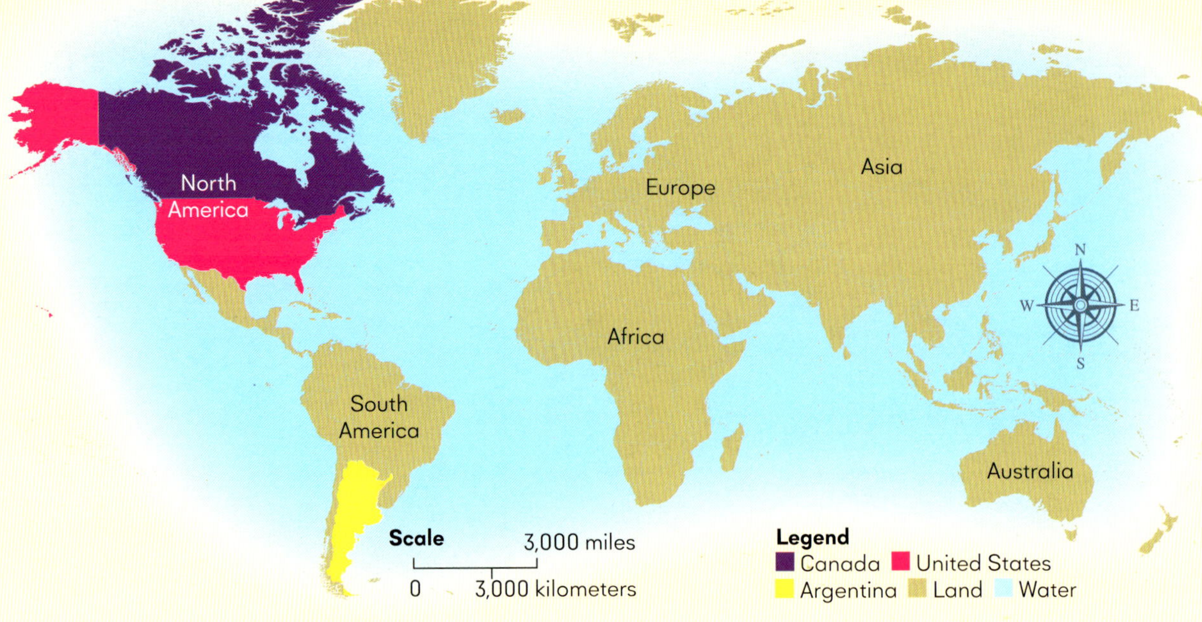

Rattlesnakes are only found in North and South America. They live as far north as Canada and as far south as Argentina. They make their homes in deserts, prairies, forests, and swamplands.

Rattlesnake Range

North America

South America

Rattlesnake Habitats

Desert

Forest

Grassland

Wetland

Prairie Rattlesnake

The prairie rattlesnake lives on the prairies of the United States and Canada. This snake often lives underground in prairie dog tunnels. It is safe and cool there. When prairie rattlesnakes are hungry, they can catch a prairie dog for a quick meal.

Eastern Diamondback Rattlesnake

Eastern diamondbacks can weigh up to 10 pounds (4.5 kilograms). These snakes are skilled swimmers but are typically found in grasslands and forests. They live in the southeastern United States.

South American Rattlesnake

The South American rattlesnake is also known as the tropical rattlesnake. This snake's venom is very strong. It can cause blindness and death. South American rattlesnakes live as far north as Mexico and as far south as Argentina.

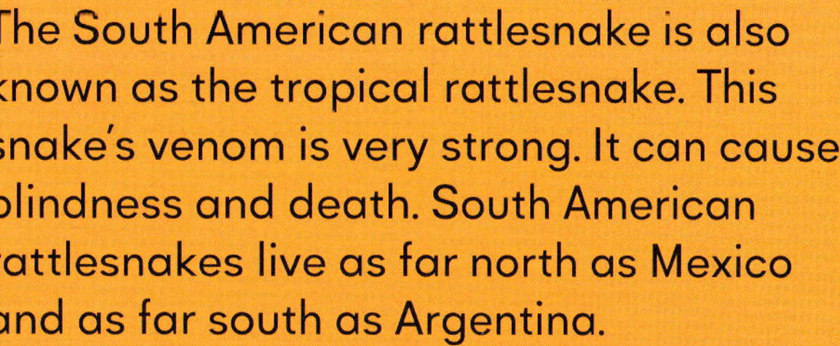

On the Hunt

Rattlesnakes hunt at night. They are **carnivores**. Rattlesnakes typically eat lizards, rats, mice, birds, and eggs. Larger snakes eat rabbits and squirrels. A rattlesnake's heat pits can detect heat from other animals from 30 feet (9 m) away, even in the dark. Once a rattlesnake detects its **prey**, it strikes and bites it with its fangs.

Rattlesnakes can sense tiny temperature differences using their pits.

Rattlesnake fangs are like needles. Venom flows through them. This venom **paralyzes** the rattlesnake's prey. A rattlesnake swallows its meals whole and headfirst.

If a rattlesnake eats a large meal, such as a rat, it will not have to eat for another two weeks.

Keeping Safe

A rattlesnake's predators include other snakes as well as foxes, eagles, and humans. When threatened, rattlesnakes will try to hide. If the rattlesnake is discovered, it will then try to get away.

If a rattlesnake cannot flee, it will hiss and rattle a warning with its tail. The rattle pieces click against each other, making a buzzing sound. Often, this will scare predators away. If the predator does not leave, the rattlesnake will bite.

Kingsnakes often hunt and eat rattlesnakes. They are able to resist rattlesnake venom.

A rattlesnake can strike in less than 0.5 seconds.

Threats to Rattlesnakes

Today, rattlesnakes face several threats to their survival. Habitat loss is one of the threats rattlesnakes face. Rattlesnake homes and hunting grounds are being destroyed. People are building towns, farms, and highways in their place. Some rattlesnakes have nowhere to live and no food to eat. Many snakes are killed as they cross busy highways.

Timber rattlesnakes, while common in many parts of the United States, are endangered in states including Vermont and Ohio.

Some rattlesnakes are hunted because people are afraid of them. Others are hunted for their skin, meat, and venom. In some places in the United States, a competition called a "rattlesnake roundup" is held. Hunters try to catch and kill the most rattlesnakes. Large numbers of rattlesnakes die each year. Although many rattlesnake populations are stable, some are considered endangered. In Canada, rattlesnakes are protected by law. In the United States, some rattlesnake species are also protected.

Tancitaran dusky rattlesnakes are considered endangered. They are found in only five locations in Mexico.

SNAKE BITES

Only about **5 people** in the United States die from snake bites each year.

Tens of thousands of rattlesnakes are hunted **each year** in "rattlesnake roundups."

ACTIVITY
Create a Snake

There are many different kinds of snakes in the world. They all have certain features in common. However, each snake also has its own unique features. They help the snake live in its home.

Make your own snake by answering the following questions:

1. What is your snake called?
2. Where does it live?
3. What features does it share with other snakes?
4. What features help it live in its home? How do these features do this?
5. What does your snake look like?
6. Use a pencil or pen to draw your snake living in its home. Make sure to include all of its features.

Supplies needed for this activity

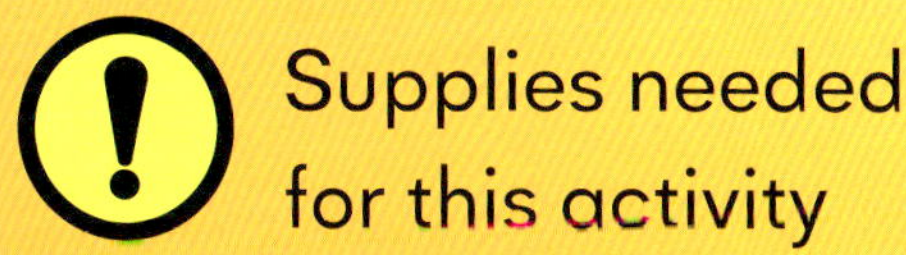

Pencil
or pen
Eraser
Paper

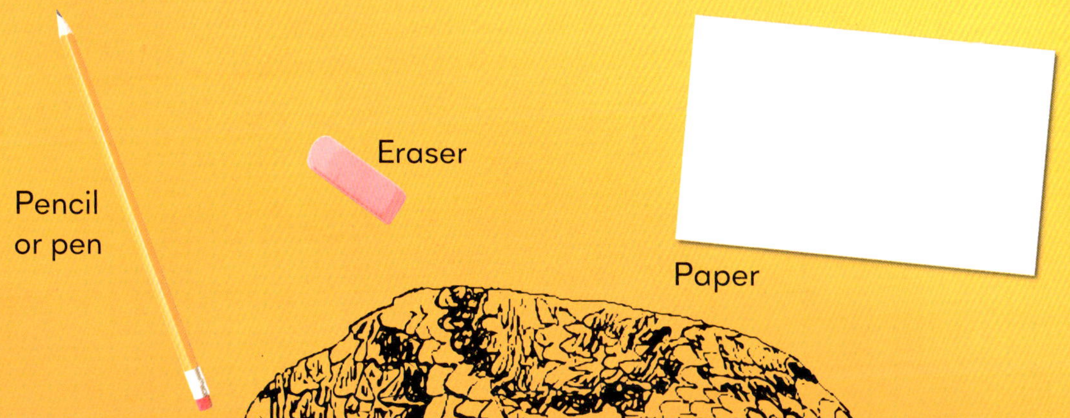

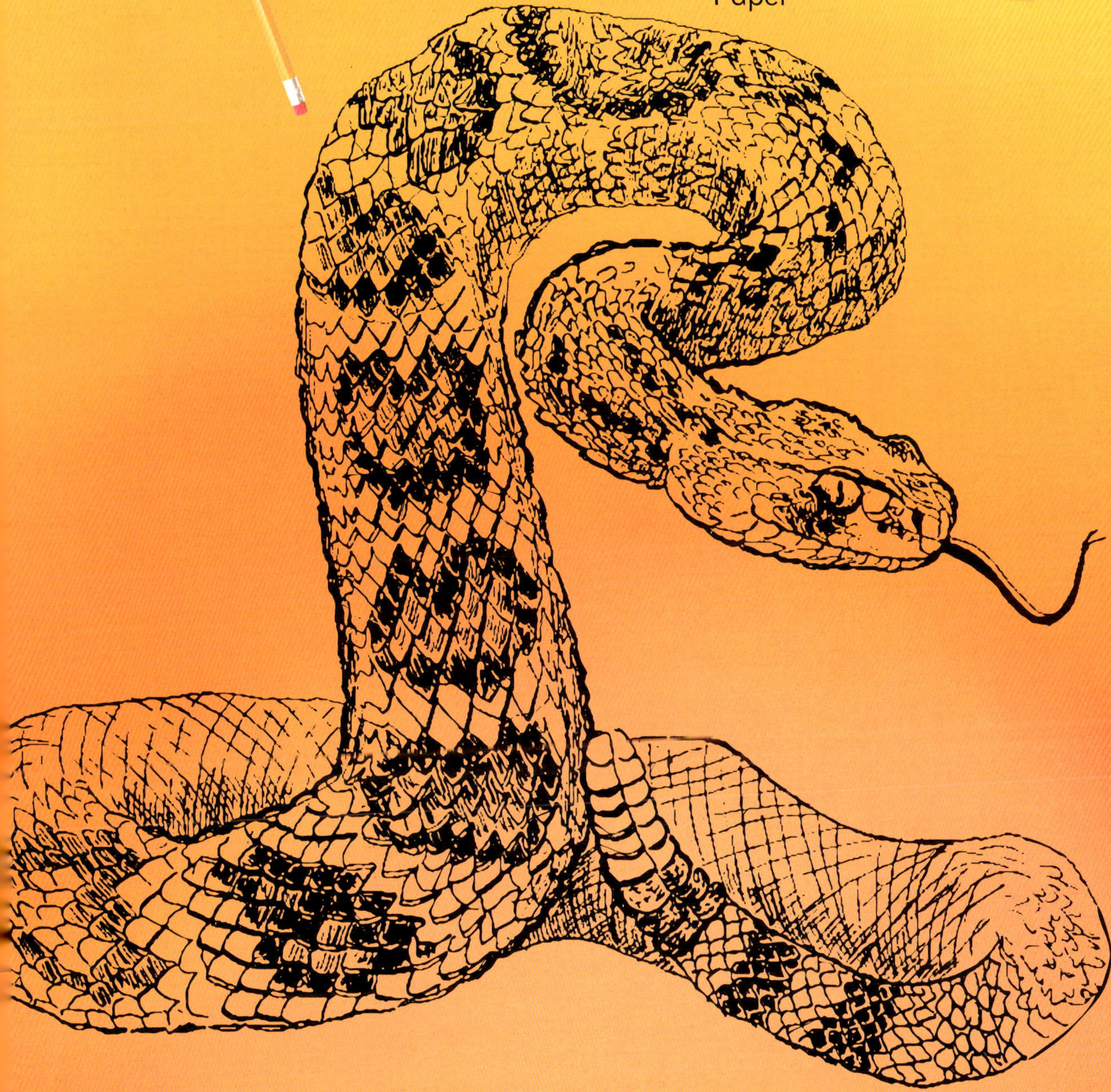

RATTLESNAKE QUIZ

How well do you know your rattlesnakes? Take this short quiz to find out.

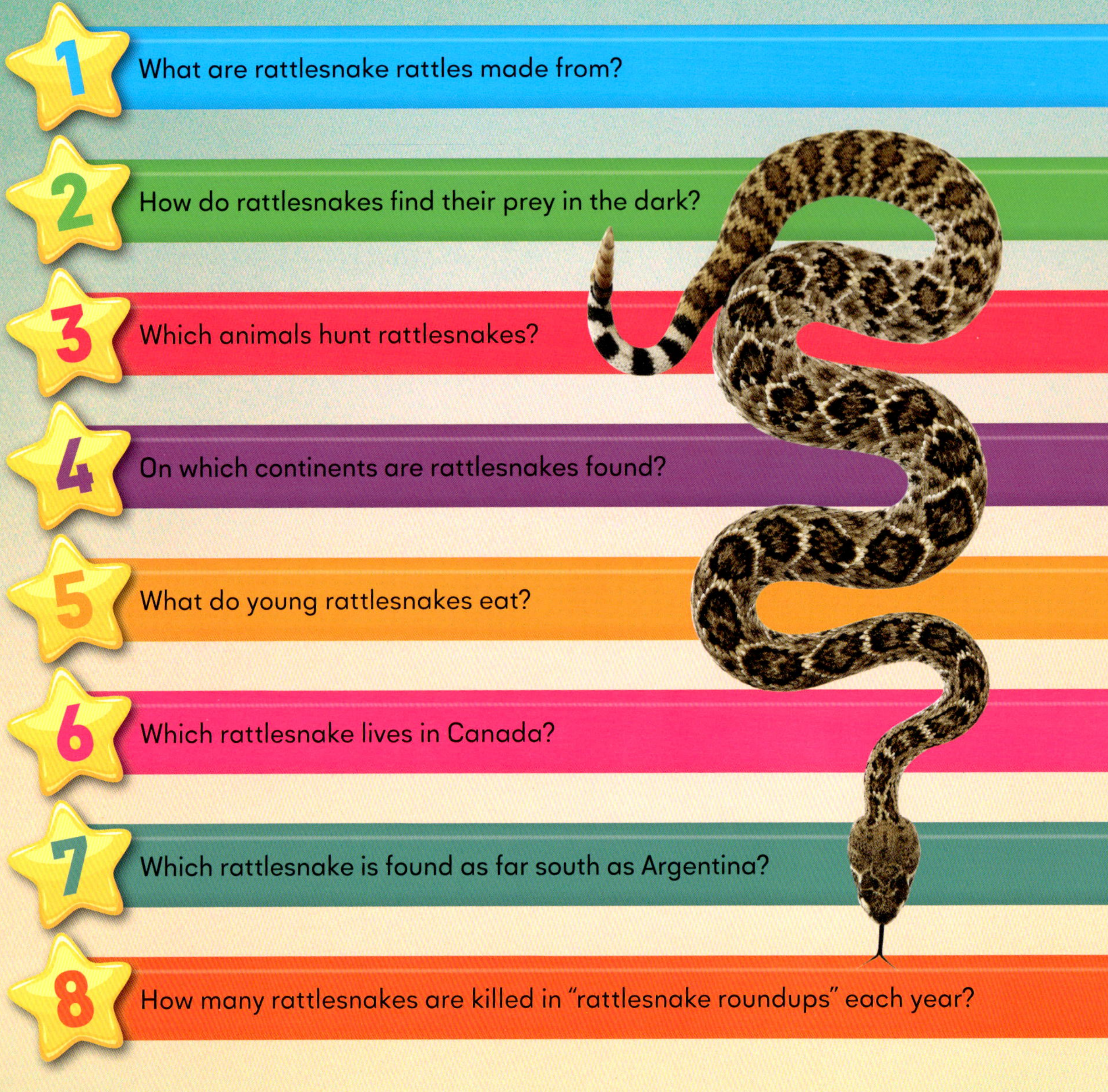

1. What are rattlesnake rattles made from?
2. How do rattlesnakes find their prey in the dark?
3. Which animals hunt rattlesnakes?
4. On which continents are rattlesnakes found?
5. What do young rattlesnakes eat?
6. Which rattlesnake lives in Canada?
7. Which rattlesnake is found as far south as Argentina?
8. How many rattlesnakes are killed in "rattlesnake roundups" each year?

ANSWERS

1. Keratin **2.** Heat pits **3.** Foxes, eagles, humans, and other snakes, such as kingsnakes **4.** North and South America **5.** Lizards and other small animals **6.** The prairie rattlesnake **7.** The South American rattlesnake **8.** Tens of thousands

Key Words

adaptations: changes in animals or plants that make them better able to survive in their homes

carnivores: animals that only eat meat

cold-blooded: an animal with blood that changes with the temperature of the animal's surroundings

fangs: sharp, pointed teeth

habitat: the place where a plant or animal lives

hibernate: to sleep or rest for a long period of time

keratin: the material that makes fingernails

mate: a member of a pair of animals that can reproduce, or have babies

paralyzes: causes a creature to be unable to move

predators: animals that hunt other animals

prey: animals that are hunted by other animals

reproduce: to have babies

segment: separate parts or sections

species: a group of closely related animals or plants

venom: a toxic chemical produced by some animals

Index

Get the best of both worlds.

AV2 bridges the gap between print and digital.

The expandable resources toolbar enables quick access to content including **videos**, **audio**, **activities**, **weblinks**, **slideshows**, **quizzes**, and **key words**.

Animated videos make static images come alive.

Resource icons on each page help readers to further **explore key concepts**.

Published by AV2
276 5th Avenue
Suite 704 #917
New York, NY 10001
Website: www.av2books.com

Copyright ©2022 AV2
All rights reserved. No part of this publication may be reproduced, stored in a retrieval system, or transmitted in any form or by any means, electronic, mechanical, photocopying, recording, or otherwise, without the prior written permission of the publisher.

Library of Congress Control Number: 2021940101

ISBN 978-1-7911-4145-5 (hardcover)
ISBN 978-1-7911-4146-2 (softcover)
ISBN 978-1-7911-4147-9 (multi-user eBook)

Printed in Guangzhou, China
1 2 3 4 5 6 7 8 9 0 25 24 23 22 21

062021
101120

Art Director: Terry Paulhus   Project Coordinator: John Willis

Every reasonable effort has been made to trace ownership and to obtain permission to reprint copyright material. The publisher would be pleased to have any errors or omissions brought to its attention so that they may be corrected in subsequent printings.

The publisher acknowledges Alamy, Getty Images, Minden Pictures, Shutterstock, and Wikimedia as the primary image suppliers for this title.

View new titles and product videos at www.av2books.com